Here's all the great literature in this grade level of *Celebrate Reading!*

BOOK B
Hurry, Furry Feet

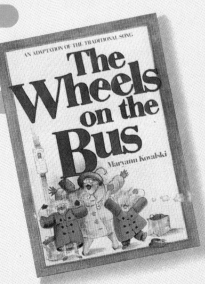

BOOK C
Our Singing Planet

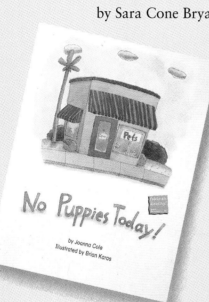

Featured Poets

N. M. Bodecker
Rowena Bennett
Mary Ann Hoberman
Lee Bennett Hopkins

Big Book & Little Book

BOOK D
My Favorite Foodles

Featured Poets

Big Book & Little Book

BOOK E

Happy Faces

BOOK F

A Canary with Hiccups

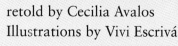

Featured Poets

Jack Prelutsky
Lee Bennett Hopkins
Shel Silverstein
Gail Kredenser
Zheyna Gay

Big Book & Little Book

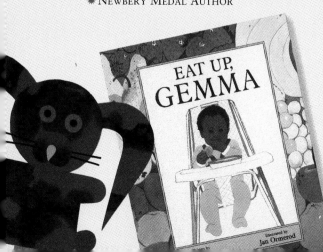

Celebrate Reading!
Big Book Bonus

It Looked Like Spilt Milk
by Charles G. Shaw

Jamberry
by Bruce Degen
✳ CHILDREN'S CHOICE

Skip to My Lou
by Nadine Bernard Westcott
✳ *REDBOOK* CHILDREN'S
PICTURE BOOK AWARD

Lazy Lion
by Mwenye Hadithi
Illustrations by
Adrienne Kennaway
✳ KATE GREENAWAY MEDAL
ILLUSTRATOR

The Cake That Mack Ate
by Rose Robart
Illustrations by
Maryann Kovalski

The Right Number of Elephants
by Jeff Sheppard

Under My Hat

About the Cover Artist

The artist Andrew Shachat painted the pictures on the
cover of this book. Mr. Shachat collects toys, especially tin
toys and robots. He says that he gets ideas for his pictures from
his collection.

ISBN 0-673-82081-5

1995 Printing
Copyright © 1993
Scott, Foresman and Company, Glenview, Illinois
All Rights Reserved.
Printed in the United States of America.

Acknowledgments appear on page 64.

345678910-RRW-9998979695

Under My Hat

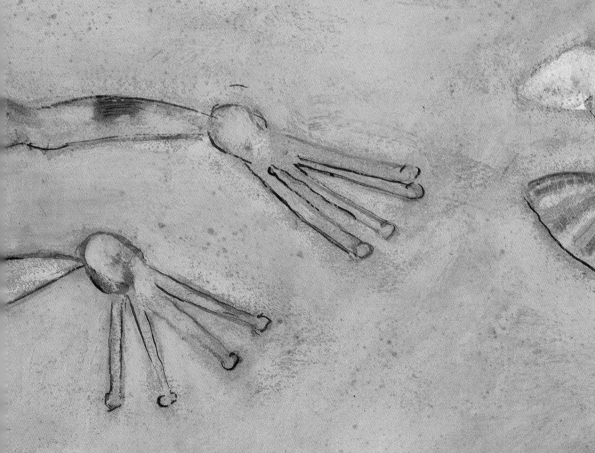

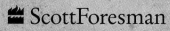
ScottForesman

A Division of HarperCollins*Publishers*

A Book to Share

Look at Me

Look at Me

So Can I

by Allan Ahlberg and Colin McNaughton

I can brush my teeth.

I can write my name.

I can read a book.

I can carry the groceries.

I can brush my teeth and
write my name and
read a book and
carry the groceries.

ONE GORILLA

by Atsuko Morozumi

Here is a list of things I love.

One gorilla.

Two butterflies among the flowers
and one gorilla.

Three parakeets in my house
and one gorilla.

Four squirrels in the woods

and one gorilla.

Five pandas in the snow
and one gorilla.

Six rabbits in a field
and one gorilla.

Seven frogs by the fence

and one gorilla.

Eight fish in the sea
and one gorilla.

Nine birds among the leaves
and one gorilla.

Ten cats in my garden
and one gorilla.

10 cats

9 birds

8 fish

7 frogs

6 rabbits

5 pandas

4 squirrels

3 parakeets

2 butterflies

But where is my gorilla?

Ah, there he is.

41

MY GORILLA

by Atsuko Morozumi

I used to live in London, England.

When I went to visit the London Zoo, I drew pictures of a very large gorilla who lived there. That gave me the idea for my book, One Gorilla.

To make all the other animals and things in my book look real, I drew from photographs and drawings.

I tried to hide the animals in my drawings. I used colors and many objects to make them hard to see.

Were you able to find them all?

Atsuko Morozumi

43

Mary Had
a Little Lamb

by Sarah Josepha Hale

photo-illustrations by Bruce McMillan

Mary had a little lamb,

Its fleece was white as snow.

And everywhere that Mary went

The lamb was sure to go.

It followed her to school one day.

That was against the rule.

It made the children laugh and play

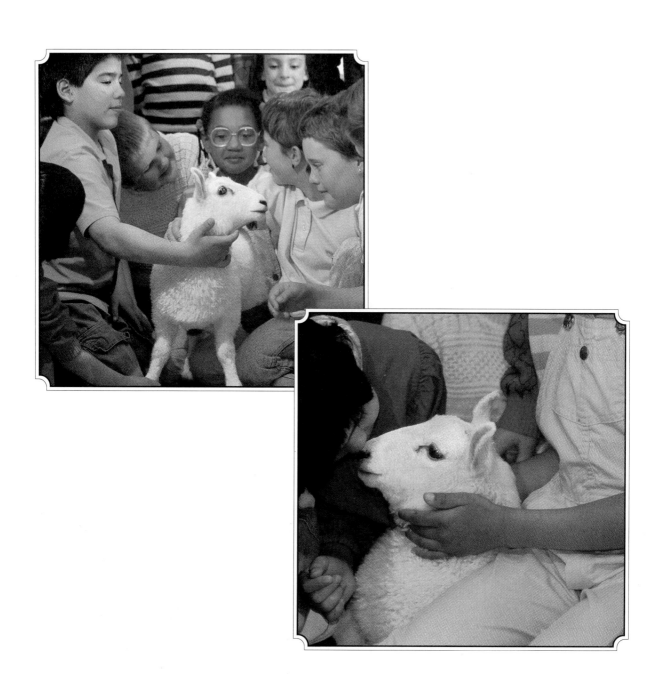

To see a lamb at school.

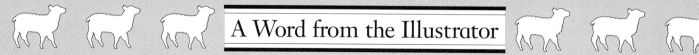

Taking Pictures of Mary and Her Lamb

by Bruce McMillan

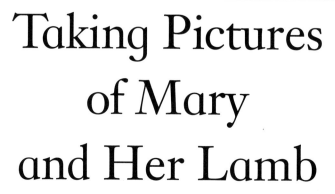

To take pictures for <u>Mary Had a Little Lamb</u>,
I needed someone to be Mary.
I found a pretty first-grade girl named
Sarah Jackson.

Second, I needed a lamb.
I found a frisky, young lamb named Argyle.

Photo: Benner McGee

Every day before I took any pictures,
Argyle got a bath. Why?
His fleece had to be "as white as snow."

I have a new sweater made from Argyle's wool.
Can you guess what color it is?

Notice

by David McCord

I have a dog,

I had a cat.

Books to Enjoy

It Looked Like Spilt Milk
by Charles Shaw

What a funny-looking thing!
Is it a bird? Is it a flower?
Read and think about what
each shape might be.

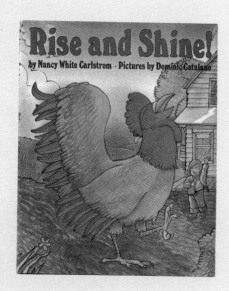

Rise and Shine!
by Nancy White Carlstrom

Join in! Talk with animals all
around the farm and all through
the year.

Things I Like
by Anthony Browne

Monkey likes to ride a bike.
Find out if he likes to do any
of your favorite things.

A Playhouse for Monster
by Virginia Mueller
Illustrations by Lynn Munsinger

Monster has his playhouse all
to himself. Why isn't he happy?

Alphabeasts
by Durga Bernhard

You can find each animal.
Then all the letters from A to Z
make a puzzle for you too!

Everything Grows
by Raffi
Photo-illustrations
by Bruce McMillan

Everything grows and grows.
Brothers, sisters, babies too.

63

Acknowledgments

Text

Page 8: *So Can I* by Allan Ahlberg and Colin McNaughton. Text copyright © 1985 by Allan Ahlberg. Illustrations copyright © 1985 by Colin McNaughton. Published in the United Kingdom by Walker Books Limited. Reprinted by permission.

Page 18: *One Gorilla* by Atsuko Morozumi. Text copyright © 1990 by Mathew Price. Illustrations copyright © 1990 by Atsuko Morozumi. Reprinted by permission of Mathew Price Ltd.

Page 42: "My Gorilla" by Atsuko Morozumi. Copyright © 1991 by Atsuko Morozumi.

Page 44: Photos from *Mary Had a Little Lamb* by Sara Josepha Hale copyright © 1990 by Bruce McMillan. All Rights Reserved. Reprinted by permission of Scholastic, Inc. Line drawing © 1990 by Bruce McMillan.

Page 56: "Taking Pictures of Mary and Her Lamb" by Bruce McMillan. Copyright © 1991 by Bruce McMillan.

Page 58: "Notice" from *One at a Time* by David McCord. Copyright © 1952 by David McCord. By permission of Little, Brown and Company.

Artists

Illustrations owned and copyrighted by the illustrator.
Andrew Shachat, cover, 1–7, 58–63
Colin McNaughton, 8–17
Atsuko Morozumi, 18–43
Bruce McMillan, 44, 56–57

Photographs

Page 43: Courtesy of Atsuko Morozumi.
Pages 44 –56: Bruce McMillan
Page 57: Benner McGee (Courtesy of Bruce McMillan.)